For you created my inmost being; you knit
me together in my mother's womb.

Psalms 139:13

Take delight in the LORD and he will give you the desires of your heart.

Of David. Praise the LORD, my soul; all my inmost being, praise his holy name.

Psalms 103:1

"Be still, and know that I am God; I will be exalted among the nations, I will be exalted in the earth."

Psalms 46:10

Children are a heritage from the LORD,
offspring a reward from him.

Psalms 127:3

A psalm of David. The LORD is my shepherd, I lack nothing.

Psalms 23:1

Of David. A psalm. The earth is the LORD's, and everything in it, the world, and all who live in it

Psalms 24:1

Surely I was sinful at birth, sinful from the time my mother conceived me.

Psalms 51:5

Whoever dwells in the shelter of the Most High will rest in the shadow of the Almighty.

Create in me a pure heart, O God, and renew a steadfast spirit within me.

Psalms 51:10

I have hidden your word in my heart that I
might not sin against you.

Psalms 119:11

He said to me, "You are my son; today I
have become your father."

I praise you because I am fearfully and wonderfully made; your works are wonderful, I know that full well

Psalms 139:14

Where can I go from your Spirit? Where
can I flee from your presence?

Psalms 139:7

Beth. How can those who are young keep their way pure? By living according to your word.

Search me, God, and know my heart; test me and know my anxious thoughts.

Psalms 139:23

And the words of the LORD are flawless, like silver
purified in a crucible, like gold refined seven times.

Psalms 12:6

The LORD has done it this very day; let us rejoice today and be glad.

Psalms 118:24

Taste and see that the LORD is good;
blessed are those who take refuge in him.

Of David. A maskil. Blessed are those whose transgressions are forgiven, whose sins are covered.

A psalm. For giving grateful praise. Shout for joy to the LORD, all the earth.

Psalms 100:1

I will instruct you and teach you in the way you should go; I will counsel you with my loving eye on you.

Psalms 32:8

Lamedh. Your word, LORD, is eternal; it stands firm in the heavens.

"Let us break their chains and throw off their shackles."

Psalms 2:3

But who delight in the law of the LORD
and meditate on his law day and night.

Psalms 1:2

Wait for the LORD; be strong and take heart and wait for the LORD.

Psalms 27:14

For he will command his angels concerning
you to guard you in all your ways

Psalms 91:11

In you, LORD, I have taken refuge; let me never be put to shame.

Psalms 71:1

Teach us to number our days, that we
may gain a heart of wisdom.

Psalms 90:12

The stone the builders rejected has
become the cornerstone

Psalms 118:22

The LORD is close to the brokenhearted
and saves those who are crushed in spirit.

Psalms 34:18

Give thanks to the LORD, for he is good;
his love endures forever.

Psalms 107:1

Let everything that has breath praise the
LORD. Praise the LORD.

Psalms 150:6

Why do the nations conspire and the peoples plot in vain?

I sought the LORD, and he answered me;
he delivered me from all my fears.

Psalms 34:4

If I had cherished sin in my heart, the Lord
would not have listened;

Psalms 66:18

I keep my eyes always on the LORD. With him at my right hand, I will not be shaken.

Psalms 16:8

Offer the sacrifices of the righteous and
trust in the LORD.

Psalms 4:5

My eyes grow weak with sorrow; they fail
because of all my foes.

Psalms 6:7

Arise, LORD! Lift up your hand, O God.
Do not forget the helpless.

Psalms 10:12

But I, by your great love, can come into your house;
in reverence I bow down toward your holy temple.

Psalms 5:7

I lie down and sleep; I wake again,
because the LORD sustains me.

Psalms 3:5

Away from me, all you who do evil, for the
LORD has heard my weeping.

Psalms 6:8

He rebukes them in his anger and terrifies them in his wrath, saying

Lead me, LORD, in your righteousness because of my enemies – make your way straight before me.

Psalms 5:8

Strike them with terror, LORD; let the nations know they are only mortals.

Psalms 9:20

For he who avenges blood remembers; he does not ignore the cries of the afflicted.

Psalms 9:12

You, LORD, hear the desire of the afflicted;
you encourage them, and you listen to their cry

Psalms 10:17

The salvation of the righteous comes from the LORD; he is their stronghold in time of trouble.

Psalms 37:39

The LORD is known by his acts of justice; the wicked are ensnared by the work of their hands.

Psalms 9:16

The LORD is King for ever and ever; the nations will perish from his land.

The LORD has heard my cry for mercy; the LORD accepts my prayer.

Psalms 6:9

The nations have fallen into the pit they have dug;
their feet are caught in the net they have hidden.

Psalms 9:15

If he does not relent, he will sharpen his sword; he will bend and string his bow.

Psalms 7:12

Arise, LORD, do not let mortals triumph; let the nations be judged in your presence.

Psalms 9:19

Defending the fatherless and the oppressed, so that mere earthly mortals will never again strike terror.

Psalms 10:18

"You will break them with a rod of iron; you will dash them to pieces like pottery."

Psalms 2:9

Fill my heart with joy when their grain and ncw wine abound.

Psalms 4:7

For I have kept the ways of the LORD; I
am not guilty of turning from my God.

Psalms 18:21

Posterity will serve him; future generations will be told about the Lord.

Psalms 22:30